The Stillwater Market Company on Water Street was doing a bustling business when John Runk took this picture on August 22, 1918.

STILLWATER

Crowded with excursionists, the steamer Ben Hur *leaves the Stillwater levee for Red Wing in 1912.*

STILLWATER

Minnesota's Birthplace
in photographs by John Runk

Text by Patricia Condon Johnston

JOHNSTON PUBLISHING, INC.
Afton, Minnesota

First Edition
Library of Congress Catalog Card Number 82-80726
International Standard Book Number 0-942934-00-8 *(softbound)*
International Standard Book Number 0-942934-01-6 *(hardbound)*

Cover

*Balloon ascensions and riverboat excursions
were popular features of summertime
celebrations in the 1880s. Stillwater was
flaunting her accomplishment by now. Good
times had arrived, and King Pine was picking
up the tab.*

for Charlie

These townsmen were photographed in their horse-drawn wagon in front of John Runk's studio at 235 South Main in the 1920s. The Valley Dri-Kleenette now has this store.

Contents

8

JOHN RUNK,
PHOTOGRAPHER
STILLWATER, MINN.

John Runk

John Runk spent a lifetime picturing Stillwater. She was his favorite subject. From her giddy youth as a lumbering town, fated for untold prosperity, to the more sober times that came after, he chased her fickle moods, caught up in her myriad fascinations. The result is a superbly detailed photographic history, an epic portrait of the town's proud past.

This early promotional photograph used by John Runk combines a formal portrait of the photographer, made at Cooper's Gallery in Stillwater in 1903 when he was twenty-five, with his dramatic eagle studio emblem.

John Runk was born May 10, 1878, in a log cabin near Menomonie, Wisconsin, the fifth child in a family of four boys and two girls born to John and Barbara Fogel Runk.

His father was a Civil War veteran who had served with the Wisconsin Volunteers at Mission Ridge, and homesteaded in Wisconsin after the war. In 1882, the family moved west to homestead in Nebraska. Two years later, when John was six, they moved to Stillwater. The Runks lived on North Second Street; their house was just below lumberman Isaac Staples's princely mansion (the present site of Pioneer Park).

When he was thirteen, John was working for the Northwest Thresher Company in Stillwater, making cones in their foundry for fifty cents a day. Later, he found employment in machine shops, and he also worked for lumbermen in the northern camps, on log drives, and at the St. Croix boom. He liked to make and sell wire costume jewelry, rings and pins, at county fairs and carnivals. He once had a job loading railroad ties onto boxcars which he described as "one of the hardest kinds of work." But by 1899, when he was twenty-one, Runk was in business for himself as a photographer.

He had shops in at least eight locations in Stillwater and called his firm the American Eagle Studio. Runk said he was the first photographer in town to use electric lights for taking portraits. He also claimed to be the first to colortint his pictures. Always interested in improving his equipment, and possessed of a mechanical bent, he made his own printer and later added an electronic timer to it.

Photographs of Stillwater and the surrounding St. Croix Valley became his specialty, indeed, his mission. He didn't drive a car, preferring to hike wherever he went, and that was frequently as far as Taylor's Falls. In the winter, he pulled his bulky equipment on a sled. Summertimes, he used a wagon. To fill out his collection, made over a period of sixty-five years, he sought out persons with earlier pictures of the area which he could copy. He would make the owner of each such picture a free print of it if he could keep one for himself. The collection he assembled this way spans close to a hundred years of Stillwater's history.

In 1937, Runk donated his first collection of 435 photographs to Stillwater's Carnegie Library. These were all eight-by-ten glossies which he made up into books, then encased in asbestos-lined metal cases that he designed to last "hundreds of years." A similar collection (but without the elaborate cases) was later given to the Washington County Historical Society. When his estate was settled, the bulk of his photographs, more than two thousand pictures, went to the Minnesota Historical Society.

John Runk and a companion at Runk's "Star Fish" hunting camp at Rice Lake, three miles below Marine on the St. Croix. Runk was a keen outdoorsman and prided himself on his prowess as a hunter, trapper, and fisherman.

John Runk remained an active photographer until his death at the age of eighty-six in 1964. His last studio was located at 103 South Main Street in the former Cosmopolitan Bank Building, where he also set up housekeeping once it became difficult for him to walk to work. He never married, and had a reputation for being a loner, but there was apparently someone special once. His personal belongings included what appeared to be a diamond engagement ring which he willed to a nephew's wife. The inventory attached to his will lists his assets at less than three thousand dollars.

There had been a single-minded purpose to John Runk's life. Stillwater was his inspiration and his obsession. With an artist's eye for detail, he delighted in his hometown's Victorian pretensions, and showcased her extravagant period finery. His legacy is Stillwater at her best, packaged for posterity.

John Runk possibly had an advertising piece for his American Eagle Studio in mind when he took this picture. The eagles are stuffed.

The Sawyer House on the corner of Second and Myrtle was a Stillwater landmark, and the social center for the city's elite. Built beginning in 1857 by Henry Sawyer from New England, it was also frequented by traveling stage celebrities, and wealthy Southerners who came to summer in Minnesota.

It changed hands several times. Sawyer found it an unprofitable venture, and Isaac Staples bought it in 1864, but held it only briefly. Much of the time it was owned by members of the Lowell family, relatives of Staples.

In 1924, the historic hotel was sold to the Mutual Hotel Company for $7,000, and the new owner contracted with a St. Paul wrecking firm to have it torn down. The Lowell Inn went up in its place.

*These men are raising a telephone pole on
Stillwater's Main Street in 1928.*

Stillwater had the first electric street cars in Minnesota in 1889 (when Twin Citians still rode horse cars), but the venture ended only a few years later in financial failure.

Dr. E. E. Allen of Davenport, Iowa, was president of the company which laid tracks for two lines, the first starting at the foot of Chestnut that went as far as Burlington and Fourth Avenue South, and the other running from the old prison to Fifth and Wilkins. The cars were built in St. Louis and were only twenty-two feet long including a three-foot platform at both ends.

Business was never brisk. The five-cent fare kept some people from using the cars. But the company managed to stay afloat until Dr. Allen began dipping into local funds to shore up his hard-pressed Davenport street car line. When Allen neglected to pay his Stillwater employees, they filed suit against him. On May 31, 1894, the sheriff foreclosed on the mortgage, and sold the property for $69,120 to Allen Curtis, the trustee for the Boston bondholders.

Fred Flint of Stillwater bought what was left of the street car line for $4,700 in 1897. He offered it to the city for $5,000, thinking town fathers might want to reactivate the line. Then reconsidering, he decided he could do better. He dug up the tracks, took down the lines, and sold the whole works for scrap.

Brownstone quarried in the Apostle Islands was used in building Stillwater's Union Depot at the foot of Myrtle Street in 1887. There were huge fireplaces in the station's waiting rooms, and a dance hall on the second floor. At one time, four railroads operated in and out of Stillwater. In later years the depot couldn't pay its keep, and it was razed in 1960 to make room for Hooley's supermarket.

Stillwater's historic post office is a classic example of the Beaux Arts style "in a Neo-Baroque mood." It now contains the Old Post Office Shops.

Horse-drawn wagons and motorized vehicles
shared Stillwater's streets when delivery men
posed for this picture outside the Minnesota
Mercantile Company in 1925. Beginning in
1888, the Minnesota Mercantile Company did
business as a wholesale and retail grocer at 401-
411 East Chestnut for more than eighty years.

Minnesota's Birthplace

Historical markers on Stillwater's Main Street, at the north and south ends of the city, welcome visitors to "The Birthplace of Minnesota." That can be confusing. Though Stillwater dates to 1843, it was not the state's first white settlement.

Orange Walker, a tanner from Vermont, heading a group of a dozen pioneer loggers, had built Minnesota's first commercial sawmill upstream at Marine in 1839. Calling themselves the Marine Lumber Company, the men had staked a claim on the unsurveyed site, put up a temporary shanty for shelter, and begun cutting timber in the northern pineries. Early in 1840, they built a substantial forty-by-twenty-eight foot log boardinghouse. Mrs. David Hone, married to one of the lumbermen, and reportedly the first white woman to reach Marine, was with the men, doing their cooking.

At Mendota, across from Fort Snelling on the west bank of the Mississippi, settlement had occurred even earlier. Fur trader Henry Sibley, twenty-four years old and already a partner in the American Fur Company, built his two-story stone residence there in 1835. Still standing, the house also served as headquarters for Sibley's far-flung fur trade empire, and was later Minnesota's first governor's mansion. A Fort Snelling census taken two years later in 1837 listed seventy-five persons in Mendota.

Nevertheless, the Stillwater claim is valid. Until 1837, most of the present state of Minnesota was Indian country. Only two relatively small parcels of land had been purchased from the Sioux. One of these was the site of Fort Snelling, built beginning in 1819; the other was located at the mouth of the St. Croix. Lieutenant Zebulon Pike, on an exploratory mission to find the headwaters of the Mississippi, had arranged this land transfer in 1805. He had never intended to defraud the Indians, yet that is exactly what happened.

The riverboat Sidney at the Stillwater levee in 1913. Extravagant excursion boats, many of them veritable floating palaces, plied the St. Croix to the end of the lumbering era.

The treaty signing with Sioux leaders took place with much ceremony under a bower made from Pike's sails near the confluence of the Minnesota and the Mississippi rivers. The land cession totaled one hundred thousand acres, and Pike estimated the property was worth $200,000. But with the Indians' consent, he left the agreement's purchase price blank; the government in Washington would supply this detail later. In the meantime, Pike distributed $200 in gifts and sixty gallons of liquor. Congress finally decided that $2,000 would do to satisfy the Indians, but more than a dozen years elapsed before even this niggardly sum was paid.

In 1837, the Indians were duped again. This time they gave up the St. Croix Valley's prize timberlands. Henry Sibley and two fellow fur traders, Lyman Warren and William Aitkin, had signed a personal treaty with the Chippewa earlier that year that allowed them to cut timber along the St. Croix and build mills at the falls above the Dalles. Annual payments in goods were to be made to the Indians for ten years. This pact was nullified, however, and the traders' lumbering plans abandoned, when the Indians ceded the land to the United States government.

Prompted by eastern lumber interests, Governor Henry Dodge of Wisconsin Territory negotiated a treaty with the Chippewa at Fort Snelling for the sale of Indian lands along the northern St. Croix on July 29, 1837. Two months later, Sioux chiefs and braves from Minnesota traveled to Washington to put their marks on a similar treaty relinquishing their rights along the southern portion of the river. When Congress ratified the agreements the next year, the pine-covered delta between the St. Croix and the Mississippi passed to white ownership.

Timber felled in Minnesota's centuries-old white pine forests was helping build the American West when this load was cut on the Kettle River for Stillwater lumbermen Martin Kane and William Sauntry in 1888.

This lumberman's mansion, built of select white pine by Roscoe F. Hersey at 416 South Fourth Street, housed three wealthy lumbermen in succession. Hersey and his family lived here from 1878 until 1890 when he sold it to John G. Nelson. In 1900, it was purchased by James Edward McGrath. There was a fire in the house in 1926, and it has since been cut down to two stories.

It appeared a fair bargain. Both treaties promised the Indians what seemed to be generous annuities in the form of money, goods, provisions, and services. The Indians were simply exchanging lands they no longer needed for the means to make them self-supporting farmers. They were also assured some measure of security. In reality, though, these treaties marked the beginning of the end of the Indians' traditional way of life.

The St. Croix Valley was only the opening wedge. Treaty upon false treaty quickly followed, consuming the Minnesota Indians' homelands. At the same time, relying on annuities, the Indians lost their incentive to provide for themselves. Historian William Folwell writes: "From that time the men would not touch a plow. They preferred to stand in the shade of a silk parasol and watch their women toil." They squandered their gold (which invariably arrived late and was less than they expected) on trinkets and whiskey. The winners were the eastern lumbermen who now held sway in the northern forests. There was still no Minnesota. But the loggers would see to that.

The timberlands were temporarily annexed to Wisconsin Territory. When Wisconsin was admitted to the Union in 1848, however, its western boundary was fixed at the St. Croix. Jubilant pioneers on the other side of the river celebrated the decision with a gala Fourth of July parade down Stillwater's Main Street.

The next month, a group of independence-minded, self-styled "citizens of Minnesota Territory" called the Stillwater Convention of 1848. Its sixty-one delegates from all parts of the orphaned region met with a single purpose in mind. The assembly was unanimous in its desire for territorial status for Minnesota. They were living, they claimed, in a no-man's land, bereft of any legal authority. Henry Sibley, who was to become the state's first governor, was elected to carry their petition to Washington, incidentally, at his own expense.

Congress dallied. There were some who would have turned the precious pinelands back to Wisconsin. There was also some discussion as to where to locate the new territorial capital. Senator Stephen Douglas from Illinois at first favored Mendota until he was convinced otherwise by Sibley. Although Mendota was essentially Sibley's personal domain, the Minnesota trader unselfishly insisted on St. Paul. He also saw to it that his bill passed both the Senate and the House. Minnesota Territory was formally organized in 1849.

The Stillwater courtroom where the plans were laid, on the second floor of lumberman John McKusick's two-story store, is gone. That building burned early in this century. The site of the territorial convention, the most important meeting ever held in the city, is marked by a bronze plaque on the present building on the southwest corner of Main and Myrtle streets.

Brewer Frank Xavier Aiple built this stone residence on his brewery premises at 734 South Main in 1868, but was accidentally killed on the property before it was completed and never occupied the house.

Stillwater's first brewer was Norbert Kimmick who was making five barrels of whiskey a week in a small still in the kitchen of his house at Third and Chestnut in 1851. The next year he built a brewery at this South Main Street location, and two years later took in Frank Aiple as a partner. When Kimmick died in 1857, Aiple married Mrs. Kimmick. The brewery burned the next year and Aiple was rebuilding it at the time he fell to his death on November 5, 1868. Mrs. Aiple married a third brewer, Herman Tepass, the following month, and the brewery went on supplying Stillwater saloons for many years.

Respectable Beginnings

For nearly half a century, townspeople turned out to see the annual St. Patrick's Day play given by a cast from St. Michael's Catholic Church. Three generations of parishioners took part in them over the years. Players in 1912 included, left to right: William Ratican, George Carroll, Anna O'Neal, Tom Curtis, Bud Sexton, Alice Donahue, Mary McAlpine, Grace White, James Clapperton, Henry Rice, and Johnnie Allen.

John McKusick, Elam Greeley, Elias McKean, and Calvin Leach were Stillwater's founding fathers. All were under thirty and had left eastern homes to make their separate ways west, and find employment at the St. Croix Falls lumber mill.

In the spring of 1843, heavy rains put them in business for themselves.

The downpour was such that it broke the log-holding boom above the mill, sending 400,000 feet of logs hurtling down the swollen river to the quieter waters of Lake St. Croix. Some of these logs were caught up by a canny riverman (thought by some historians to have been Stephen Hanks, Abraham Lincoln's cousin) and rafted down the Mississippi to a southern market, saving the mill owners from financial ruin. That was the first log raft to negotiate the Mississippi. Other logs, hung up along the banks of the St. Croix, were given to McKusick and the others as part of their wages.

Before the end of the year the four were building a sawmill on the west shore of Lake St. Croix on a claim bought for $300 from Jacob Fisher, a carpenter with the lumber company at the Falls. Fisher's was the first land claim in Stillwater. He also showed the men how to dam the upland lake, now named for McKusick, and funnel its flow down a long wooden overhead viaduct to power the mill's machinery.

McKusick named the settlement Stillwater. He was referring, he said, to the serenity of Lake St. Croix at the mill's doorstep. The site was ideal. Stillwater would thrive, beyond every expectation, because of its location.

This was the scene at Fourth and Hickory following what John Runk called a "cloudburst" on May 9, 1894.

In 1845, Nathaniel Fish Moore, the eminent president of New York City's Columbia College, stopping at Stillwater enroute to see the Falls of St. Anthony, described the village as having "a saw mill, a tavern, a country merchant's store, and some half dozen wooden houses." Three years later, there were five stores fronting the main street, two hotels, "a flourishing school," and about twenty-five "very neat and well-finished buildings." All were dependent upon the sawmill.

Stillwater's first post office operated out of a corner in McKusick's store beginning in 1845. Before that, mail was a happenchance thing, carried by anyone going to or coming from Prairie du Chien. Elam Greeley was Stillwater's postmaster; the next year, McKusick succeeded him.

McKusick's three partners sold out to him in 1844, and his was the only sawmill in town until the early 1850s. Most of his lumber was shipped downstream to St. Louis because Minnesota was too sparsely settled to provide much of a home market. By 1849, there were only 609 people in Stillwater. The population of Minnesota Territory that year was 4,680. But McKusick prospered. In 1852, his fortunes increased, again the result of torrential spring rains.

Lake McKusick had filled to its rim by mid-May and the surrounding sandy bluffs were soaked to the consistency of "children's mud pies" when one thunderstorm too many burst the dam keeping back the flow of water in the channel leading to McKusick's mill. The flood that ensued washed away the high banks on either side of the channel, and great masses of soft earth were sent down into the rushing current. One slide followed another and the deluge gained momentum as it headed for the waterfront. One townsman was sure he was seeing the end of the world. Trees were uprooted and boulders dislodged; barns, tenements, and shops were swept away. When it was over, the lower story of McKusick's mill was filled with mud and muck, and his machinery was buried.

The lumberman thought himself ruined. Instead, the calamity worked to his advantage. Once dug out, his machinery was still usable. Better still, the landslide had greatly improved the waterfront by depositing up to ten feet of new soil over about six acres. (This area extended from about Second Street down to the lake, and from Myrtle to just north of Commercial Street.) Land that sold for $1.25 an acre before the storm now brought $50 to $500. Three years later, the *St. Croix Union* reported that the sawmill's properties could not be bought for $50,000.

A tall, gaunt pipe-smoker who reminded people of Abraham Lincoln, McKusick remained one of the town's leading citizens for more than fifty years. At one time he owned most of the north half of Stillwater. During the 1860s, he served four years as state senator. Originally from Cornish, Maine, he also lured his five brothers to Stillwater.

Jonathan McKusick, familiarly known as "Cap," came in 1845. Stillwater's first cat came with him. Boxed for the journey, it appeared to be dead on arrival. "Cap" was holding an inquest over its remains when onlookers noticed signs of life. Sufficient blood-letting restored the cat to consciousness, and it lived several years thereafter, a terror to the rats in Stillwater. Jonathan McKusick was always known for his genial good humor, and held various offices in the city. Following the Sioux Uprising in 1862, he marched with Sibley's expedition in pursuit of the renegade Indians.

Heaped together in wild confusion ("like a giant's game of jackstraws," said James Taylor Dunn), this spectacular log jam piled up in the narrow channel of the Dalles below Taylor's Falls in 1884. The year before, crews worked fifty-seven days with the help of steamboats to unlock a similar jam.

A second brother, William McKusick, was also prominent in the business and social affairs of the community. He was a member of the fifth territorial house, and several times a state senator. In the early 1870s, he was a member of the firm of McKusick, Anderson & Company which built a large sawmill at Houlton, opposite Stillwater.

Noah McKusick came to Stillwater with logging on his mind too, but left shortly afterwards for the gold fields in California.

Royal McKusick settled permanently in Stillwater in 1848, but died a few years later leaving little but a "large and respectable family."

The youngest McKusick brother, Ivory, twenty when he arrived in 1847, worked first in John's mill, and was later a prison guard. Ivory McKusick also became an adept financier, and profited handsomely from government contracts during the Civil War. The house he built in Stillwater in 1866, a splendid French Second Empire cottage, still stands at 504 North Second Street.

Photographed in 1885, this portion of the extensive Hersey Bean lumber yards was built on pilings over the St. Croix river.

Alexander "Sandy" McDougal was Stillwater's answer to Paul Bunyan. He worked sixty consecutive winters in the woods, thirty of them as walking boss for Isaac Staples, and came down the river on forty-nine log drives. "The King of the St. Croix Lumberjacks," they called him, and the title was rightfully his.

He was both lion and lamb to those who knew him. The story is told that he once stopped a log drive to recover the body of a youth who had drowned from Marine, toted it back through seven miles of trackless forest to camp, then sent it on with a package of the boy's clothes and effects to his mother for burial.

When the drive reached Marine, the mother was waiting for Sandy in the wanigan.

"Are you Sandy McDougal?" she demanded. He was, he said. "And are you the one who sent me his clothes?" she wanted to know. When Sandy again replied in the affirmative, she was furious.

"Well, I think you must be a mean, dirty skunk to steal his hat. I paid three dollars for it and it was brand new. I want that hat or you got to pay me for it." Too kind to do otherwise, McDougal handed over the money for the hat.

When a bunch of hooligans later poked fun at him over the incident in a bar, however, they were up against a different man. Calmly wiping the beer from his whiskers, he faced the lot of them and threw them out of the place.

Sandy McDougal retired from the woods at the age of seventy-six in 1919, and moved to a piece of land he owned near Mora. He died five years later, and is buried in St. Michael's Cemetery in Bayport, the final resting place of numerous Valley lumbermen.

Opportunity Beckons

Stillwater took precious little time becoming the lumber industry's headquarters in the St. Croix Valley. Within ten years after McKusick built his sawmill, there were five others in town. In 1854, the famous steam-operated Hersey and Staples mill moved in. Backed by eastern capital, it reportedly cost $80,000 and was said to be the finest sawmill in the West. Its resident owner, Isaac Staples, was an ingenious Yankee who would shape young Stillwater to his liking, and make himself the town's first millionaire in the process.

Staples was a minister's son, born in Topsham, Maine, in 1816. By rights, he was his father's property until he was twenty-one, but at eighteen, he "bought his time" from his parent for $360 and hired out as a lumberjack on the Penobscot River. He was in Old Town, Maine, engaged in general merchandising when he was twenty. The next year he was back to lumbering, this time doing business with Samuel Freeman Hersey, the man who would help finance the Stillwater mill.

In 1853, while Hersey stayed behind in Maine, Staples traveled to the St. Croix Valley to investigate reports concerning the area's virgin stands of white pine. Staples was convinced of the wealth to be made in these forests, and returned to Maine where he secured investment capital to build a mill. The next year he moved his family to Minnesota.

The Hersey, Staples mill was the first in Stillwater to have a gang saw or a circular saw. Its gang saw held twenty parallel saws in one frame. The minimum output of a circular saw, usually 5 to 5 1/2 feet in diameter and sometimes called a rotary or rip saw, was 1,000 feet per hour. With these, and three upright saws, the mill could cut 125,000 feet of lumber in twenty-four hours. Slabs and sawdust, then considered waste, fueled the mill's enormous steam engines.

Hersey, Staples and Company controlled every aspect of their lumbering business. Within seven years of his arrival in Minnesota, Isaac Staples had bought two hundred thousand acres of pine forests on the

St. Croix and its tributaries. (The going rate was $1.25 per acre.) The company hired its own logging crews. It was a wholesale distributor and sold at retail as well. The firm also branched out into supporting industries: merchandising, transportation, and banking.

Isaac Staples's general store opened in Stillwater in 1854 with an inventory of dry goods, clothing, and groceries. He insisted on high quality stock. Minnesota, he wrote back East, was "a poor market for poor goods." His newspaper advertisements that year listed shipments of buffalo and seal-skin overcoats, "heavy Buffalo overshoes," "100 per Lumberman's Blankets," "heavy fringed black and colored shawls," skates, "a large lot of superior pocket and table cutlery," ledgers, journals, and day books, along with steel pens and "Black-Ink wafers," guns of different kinds, "a good assortment of paint brushes," and "seamless meal sacks." For gentlemen, he had "fine dress frock coats," black satin or cashmere vests, "heavy satinette pants," and gold and silver watches. Lumberjacks could find duck overalls, red and blue flannel shirts, "heavy wool drawers," wool socks and mittens, and "Lumberman's heavy boots."

A second giant on the local lumbering scene was F. Schulenburg and A. Boeckeler and Company. These two men were from St. Louis where they operated a successful sawmill and lumber yard. Boeckeler came north to oversee the company's business in Stillwater, while Schulenburg remained in charge at St. Louis. The first sawmill they built in Stillwater in 1854 was replaced a few years later with a larger one equipped with two gang saws, one with eighteen saws, the other with twenty-four. For many years, the Schulenburg, Boeckeler firm was the biggest log cutter in Stillwater. Virtually every board from this mill went to St. Louis. A local demand for lumber was growing, of course, but the town still sold most of its prodigious output downstream in Iowa, Illinois, and Missouri.

Isaac Staples's Italianate residence was built in 1871 atop the city's North Hill, overlooking the lumberman's riverfront domain. Designed by St. Paul architect A. M. Radcliffe, it was reputedly the finest house in the state.

Its eighteen rooms included a third-floor ballroom, and Staples grew exotic fruits in an attached conservatory. A barn and a carriage house stood on the grounds, as did at least two smaller houses for servants and family members. Vineyards were planted on the property's southern and eastern slopes. All of this was enclosed by an ornate iron fence, one length of which still stands along North Second Street.

After Staples died in 1898, the house remained empty for several years until it was finally leveled. Since 1935, the property has been the site of Pioneer Park, named for Staples and his contemporaries.

There was no log boom at first, and lumbering along the St. Croix in its earliest years was a catch-as-catch-can affair. Sloughs made do as collection points where the logs were either made into rafts to be floated downriver or sorted and assigned to local sawmills. As the number of loggers increased, so did the confusion.

In 1851, eight valley lumbermen, among them Orange Walker from Marine, and John McKusick from Stillwater, incorporated as the St. Croix Boom Company in an attempt to bring order to the growing chaos. At a point six miles below Taylor's Falls and approximately two miles upstream from Osceola, huge piers were sunk at intervals from the Minnesota shore to the foot of a long mid-channel island still known as Boom Island, and similarly, from the head of the island to the Wisconsin shore. Floating timbers chained between the piers caught and contained logs for sorting and measuring and rigging into rafts. From the beginning, though, the new boom posed problems.

The slough on the Minnesota side was so narrow that the river was frequently plugged with logs. That violated the boom company's charter which required that it keep a channel open to traffic. When the steamer *Asia* was unable to forge her way through oncoming logs in 1853, the company was forced to pay the cost of transporting its freight to Taylor's Falls. Stillwater lumbermen also found that the Osceola boom didn't meet their needs. It was too far upstream to catch the Apple River logs once they came into the St. Croix.

Three log rollers compete for prizes during a Fourth of July log rolling contest in Stillwater in 1903. Independence Day was the biggest holiday of the year. The log drives were usually in, and everybody quit work for a day or two to celebrate.

Once he gained control of the boom company, it was Isaac Staples who decided to build a new boom two miles above Stillwater in 1856. Schulenburg and Boeckeler bought stock in the organization as did other mill owners along the river, eventually as far downstream as Winona. Ideally positioned between steep bluffs where long narrow islands divide the river into several channels, the new boom became a Stillwater institution. It was the giant heart that pumped this lumbertown's lifeblood.

As the demand for lumber increased, the boom took on immense proportions, and at one time extended a distance of nine miles. During peak years, the boom employed four hundred men on a duty shift, sorting, scaling, and rafting timber. Logs stamped with at least two thousand different owner marks passed through the boom. On shore, twenty buildings were needed to carry on the company's transactions and house and feed its workers. Up until the early years of this century, most every man in Stillwater (including photographer John Runk) worked one time or another at the boom.

River traffic still sometimes came to a halt. The new boom provided canals for steamboats to use when the main channel was blocked, but the millions of logs pouring annually out of the northern pineries clogged these too. Once, when shipping had been stopped for fifty-seven days, damages against the boom company were estimated at $146,525. But the St. Croix was a lumberman's river, and as long as the forests lasted no one ever seriously challenged timber's right-of-way.

This Sunday portrait of the Ann River Logging Company camp was taken by photographer S. C. Sargent of Taylor's Falls in 1892. The Ann River is in Kanabec County; it flows into the Snake River which comes into the St. Croix near Pine City. The Ann River Logging Company was a Weyerhaeuser enterprise, managed by William Sauntry, with offices in the Lumbermen's Exchange Building in Stillwater.

afts and River Pilots

Both logs and lumber were rafted downstream from Stillwater. Log rafts were commonly made up of eight to ten strings of logs fastened side by side, each string being sixteen feet across and about four hundred feet in length. In later years, the best of these rafts measured four or five acres in size. Lumber rafts differed only in that the lumber was arranged in cribs or heavy crates, each sixteen feet wide and thirty-two feet long. A lumber raft plying the Mississippi might contain as many as two hundred cribs.

Rafting was never easy work. The earliest rafts were propelled from Stillwater to St. Louis by oarsmen, and a lot could go wrong on the river. Storms and reefs and rapids all claimed their toll. It took a quick-witted hard-working riverman to get his raft to market intact.

Lake St. Croix and Lake Pepin were especially testy and dangerous bodies of water. When the winds were right, the first rafts were sometimes sailed through these lakes, using blankets for sails. It made good sense to hurry through them. One veteran lumberman writes of seeing the west shore of Lake Pepin, from Lake City to Read's Landing, "white from broken lumber, when three lumber rafts were broken to pieces and rendered entirely valueless in a storm." There were also times when the only way to move a raft was to put all hands on shore and pull it with a hand line. This was called cordelling, and the crew was lucky to make four miles progress in a sixteen-hour day. Stephen Hanks, who rafted lumber from John McKusick's Stillwater mill to St. Louis beginning in the 1840s, said it once took him two weeks just to pass through the two lakes, a distance of fifty-seven miles.

ne steamer Kalitan *and barge* Markatana *at e Stillwater levee on July 19, 1919. The old ooden pontoon draw bridge is seen in the ckground.*

Further downstream, in Iowa and Illinois, the Upper and Lower Rapids terrorized raft crews. The Upper Rapids, beginning at Le Claire, were fourteen miles long with a fall of twenty-two feet. Rock Island lay at the bottom, and there was no channel cut through the rock as there is now. The Lower Rapids reached twelve miles from Montrose to Keokuk and likewise required an expert river pilot to steer clear of disaster.

A good pilot was worth his weight in gold, and mill owners knew it. His river savvy meant their survival, and they paid him accordingly. Crewmen signed on for thirty-five dollars for a trip downriver (plus return fare), but a pilot's wages were as high as five hundred dollars a month in the early 1850s. Idolized by young boys and admired by the ladies, the river pilot became a folk hero in his own generation. Easy to pick out, he was the dashing fellow dressed in "French calf boots, black cassimere trousers, red flannel shirt of extra fine knitted goods, a large black silk necktie, tied in a square knot with flowing ends, and a soft, wide-brimmed black or white hat."

Towboats were introduced on the river in 1851, and subsequently revolutionized rafting. The *Caleb Cape* began her work that year, pushing rafts from behind. The regular charge for taking a raft from Stillwater to Read's Landing below Lake Pepin was ten dollars per string. In 1855, Captain W. H. Carbut advertised in the *St. Anthony Messenger* that his steamboat, the *Dubuque,* was towing rafts through Lake St. Croix and Lake Pepin. It would be some years, however, before anyone attempted to run a raft with a steamboat in the Mississippi proper. For the time being, the use of towboats was confined to the two lakes.

John Runk photographed these remnants of Slab Alley in 1932. Built tight against the bluffs south of Stillwater, the two-block long row of millworkers' houses was later obliterated by Highway 95. Bing Crosby's mother, Catherine Harrigan, was born on Slab Alley, and baptized in St. Michael's Catholic Church on February 11, 1873.

Sinners and Polite Society

Young Stillwater was more than a little on the wild side. With half her population "unmarried men and bachelors," she could hardly be otherwise.

Come springtime, when the lumberjacks descended on the town after six months confinement in the winter camps, decent citizens locked their doors. Whiskey ran freely in the town's dozen saloons while the men warmed up to their freedom, proving their prowess with their fists. Some went on days-long drunken binges, "a sort of jollification" one reporter called it. Others hightailed it across the lake to take their pleasure in the "sink-holes of sin" at St. Petersburgh (now Houlton), bordellos run by the likes of Red Nell and Perry the Pimp that relied on the Stillwater jacks to keep them in business. (The Victorian, the sedate red brick house at 109 East Myrtle in Stillwater that now sells women's clothing, also once did a stint as a house of prostitution.)

The editors of the *Democrat*, one of two local papers, were frankly worried at the prospects of the town's young men. "Where will you find one in a dozen who promises well for manhood?" they asked. "Plenty can be found who will grow up into rowdies, shoulderhitters and drunkards. And what better can we expect of any community that encourages gaming, drinking, and rowdyism?" Author Stewart Holbrook called Stillwater "Minnesota's earliest whoopee-town."

But there was a flip side to Stillwater's character. Despite her madcap behavior (attributable to growing pains, no doubt), she was also acquiring some social graces. Many of her working men might have been unschooled laborers, but the town also had a liberal sprinkling of educated citizenry, mainly lawyers, physicians, and ministers. These men and their wives brought refinement to the community in good measure.

Stillwater's many church towers and steeples pierce its picturesque skyline. This is Third Street, looking south, in 1887.

Reverend E. A. Greenleaf was conducting Episcopal services in Elam Greeley's house on Main Street in 1846, and Presbyterian missionary W. T. Boutwell was preaching in Stillwater by the next year. Within ten years, there were six churches of various denominations and an active Washington County Bible Society.

Stillwater's educational system was likewise started early. Sarah Louise Judd was teaching school (for nine pupils) during the summer of 1846. Her first classes were held in a vacant dwelling, but that same season a separate schoolhouse was erected, paid for by public contributions. The school district was formally organized in 1850, and in the ensuing years Stillwater pioneers built some of the most attractive schools in the state.

Besides church and school, the town also had numerous social organizations. Freemasonry came to Stillwater in 1850, with the establishment of "St. John's Lodge, No. 1," and a group of Odd Fellows commenced a lodge of their own the following year. A German Turnverein, and a German singing society were started in 1859. That same year, the Stillwater Library Association (the present Carnegie Library evolved from it) was formed to care for congressional papers and records received from U. S. Senator Henry Rice.

Any way one looked at it, the town was off to a running start. Self-confident and lusty, and already the capital of lumbering on the St. Croix, Stillwater had hitched her bandwagon to good times ahead.

Greeley School, on Greeley near Olive, was one of three elementary schools built in Stillwater in the early 1870s. Later-day pupils posed for this springtime portrait on May 15, 1910.

The State Penitentiary

Stillwater had high hopes once of becoming the capital of Minnesota, but when the territorial legislature convened in 1851, St. Paul was awarded that distinction. Stillwater received another prize of sorts: the state penitentiary. Congress appropriated the funds, $20,000 for the facility which was considered a necessity in a new territory, and a three-story prison house with two "dungeons" was built in Battle Hollow (the site of a bloody encounter between the Sioux and the Chippewa fourteen years earlier).

At first, prison inmates were garbed in hickory-cloth shirts and gray pants, with red and blue jackets and blanket wool caps. One half of each prisoner's head was also shaved. When numerous prisoners thus dressed escaped with amazingly little difficulty, "penitentiary stripes" were introduced in 1860 to make escapees easier to identify. Inmates were issued hip jackets, trousers, and skull caps of heavy blanket cloth with alternating black and white horizontal stripes, and the regulation uniforms continued to be used within the prison walls until 1921.

The prison's first warden, Frank R. Delano, appointed in 1853, knew little of prison management. During one ten-month period in 1856, eight inmates pried, sawed, or tunneled their way out of confinement. When there was a public outcry, Delano contended that the blame lay with the construction of the prison rather than his administration. Its walls and buildings, he pointed out, were not "of the most approved and substantial kind." But there were no night guards, and in 1858, four more prisoners made their way over the wall while the guard was attending church services.

The Minnesota State Prison on North Main Street was one of young Stillwater's most striking features. The three Younger brothers, who all received life sentences in 1876 for their part in the Northfield bank robbery and the murder of cashier Joseph L. Heywood, were incarcerated here. The warden's house on the left is the only surviving original building. It is now the Washington County Historical Museum.

Delano turned other inmates loose himself. By law, he was required to take in temporary prisoners from Minnesota counties lacking adequate jail facilities. Room and board for these inmates, three dollars a week and payable in advance, was charged to the counties requesting their incarceration. When these accounts became delinquent, however, Delano felt no responsibility to go on supporting the men. If a man's keep was not paid, no matter his crime (and more than once the charge was murder), Delano simply put him out on the street.

Delano also realized that the prison contained a captive supply of cheap labor, and set up a profitable personal business on the prison grounds. Taking advantage of the regulation that said inmates were to be kept busy from sunrise to sunset (with a half hour allowed for each meal), the warden spent eight thousand dollars out of his own pocket for steam-operated machinery, and put the men to work making shingles, doors, sashes, flooring, wagons, and plows. He also hired fifteen Stillwater men to help with special orders. One of these commissions specified fencing for the grounds of the Capitol in St. Paul.

In 1859, after Delano's term as warden expired, John B. Stevens, a Stillwater manufacturer of shingles and blinds, leased the prison workshop from the state and took over the convict labor. The contract system of hiring out prisoners became much criticized, but it would continue at the prison until the facility closed fifty-five years later.

Stevens' mill burned in 1861, bankrupting him, and the contract for convict labor went to George Seymour and William Webster who made flour barrels. By the end of the 1860s, Dwight M. Sabin, later a United States senator, was in partnership with Seymour. Thereafter, the firm of Seymour, Sabin and Company controlled prison labor (and prison affairs in general) for the next twenty years.

The Stillwater penitentiary included fourteen cells for female prisoners, located in the front on the second floor of the main building. These inmates were photographed in the prison yard about 1910.

In 1870, prisoners produced barrels, tubs, and buckets worth $50,000 for Seymour and Sabin. The next year the firm's sales amounted to $135,000, and despite growing antagonism toward its method of operation, the company continued to grow rapidly.

It began making threshing machines in 1876, and with the new Minnesota Chief (which it called "the most successful thresher in the world"), Seymour, Sabin et al became the country's largest manufacturer of such equipment. Net profits for 1881 amounted to $300,000. The next year, Sabin reorganized the firm as the North Western Manufacturing and Car Company, and added railroad freight and passenger cars to its growing list of products.

Besides convict labor, admittedly obtained through a "very advantageous contract" with the state, the firm also employed twelve hundred civilians, mainly mechanics and machinists. They worked both inside the prison and in the sprawling manufacturing complex that grew up outside its walls.

This was not the worst of it. Through a series of bargains signed with the state, the firm acquired a virtual stranglehold on the prison itself. They received all the contracts for additions and improvements at the prison. Consequently, the amounts they paid to the state for convict labor and shop rental were less than they got back by way of the arrangement. They even decided who might and who might not be hired as guards and officers at the institution.

Stillwater bought its first fire engine, a "Silsby," for $7,375 in 1872 after the city had been visited by several devastating blazes. Stillwater's "great fire" took place the day after Christmas, 1866. Starting on Main Street near Chestnut, it consumed twelve buildings before being brought under control. A half dozen years later, on March 5, 1872, a fire broke out on the corner of Main and Nelson, burning six buildings, and leaving three families homeless. Two months after this, townsmen were testing the Silsby engine prior to purchasing it. Placing it near the lake, they were anxious to see if it could force a stream of water through 1500 feet of hose and throw it over the courthouse dome. It could and did, and a volunteer fire company of sixty volunteers was formed. The brick engine house was located on Commercial Street between Main and Second streets.

Though outrageously unfair, these practices continued at the prison until 1887 when public disgust with the inequitable system, coupled with pressure from the St. Paul Trades and Labor Assembly, prompted state lawmakers to pass legislation forbidding the use of prison labor in competition with free enterprise. The decision caused temporary problems at the prison. Four hundred inmates were idled, and the effect on their morale was said to be disastrous. This caused the legislature to change its earlier decision and half of the prisoners were allowed to go to work on a short-term basis for the Minnesota Thresher Company, a new corporation formed by stockholders of the car company. At the same time, the state started a binder twine business at the prison to employ the remainder of the men.

Decades before the demise of the old prison, it was described as not being "fit to keep hogs in, let along human beings." The buildings were damp, poorly-ventilated, and overrun with roaches. Prisoners complained of the numerous bedbugs which drove them "wild with pain and annoyance." They charged the stench of the place was "almost intolerable." Henry Wolfer, warden at the prison from 1892, repeatedly pointed out the need for new buildings to legislators. In 1905 and 1909, funds were allocated for a new state penitentiary which was built south of Stillwater at Bayport. The last of Stillwater's prisoners were transferred there in 1914, and most of the old prison buildings were demolished. The twelve-foot wall which once fronted North Main Street has been replaced by a historical marker.

Charlie Lustig ran one of the town's better saloons in the Lumbermen's Exchange Building. The three-story brick building at Chestnut and Water streets was the finest office building in Stillwater when it was built in 1890. Equipped with the most modern plumbing, heating, and lighting, it even had an elevator (described as being "a little slow on the rise"). Its tenants in its first ten years were mostly lumbermen. After that, with logging on the decline, lawyers, along with real estate and insurance firms moved into its offices. Today it also houses Stillwater's Chamber of Commerce.

Boom Years and Bust

Stillwater grew rapidly in the years following the Civil War. If there had ever been any doubt about the town's future, there was none now. The railroads were reaching into Minnesota and beyond. Stillwater firms that had once sold their lumber exclusively downriver were shipping lumber by rail as far west as Colorado. Two thousand men with five hundred teams of horses went into the woods in 1871 and harvested more than 145,000,000 feet of logs. The figure climbed to 200,000,000 feet by 1880; and at the peak of production in 1890, a record 450,000,000 board feet of lumber came through the St. Croix boom. Stillwater's population soared to 18,000. And more than a few fortunes were made.

Stillwater, shaking off the makeshift look of her youth, came of age in the most lavish attire lumbermen could afford.

Men who made their money cutting and marketing timber flaunted it in their homes. Stillwater remains a veritable museum of the delightful distractions of nineteenth-century architecture. Village forefathers had patterned their white-painted pine houses after those they remembered from the East. A trend was established, and the city came to look much like a typical New England town. Even so, none of the European-inspired architectural fads to change the face of America during the last century seemed to bypass Stillwater. Pattern books provided its carpenters with all the details they needed to concoct a plethora of picturesque and exotic designs.

Heavily bracketed squat Italian villas went up next to tall, white pine Gothic houses fairly dripping with medieval trimmings. Circumspect hip-roofed Federal homes were overshadowed by grandiloquent French imperial styles with more fashionable mansard roofs. Already elaborate facades were further embellished with cupolas and campaniles, turrets and tracery.

These logs were shipped by rail from Virginia, Minnesota, to Stillwater in 1903 and 1904 to be made into rafts and floated down the Mississippi. John Runk identified the men on the logs from left to right as Peter Gustafson, Charles Jackson, Pat Fitzgerald, Charles Johnson, Charles Swansen, John Magnusen, Ed Nelson, Oscar Gustafson, and Peter Johnson.

One prominent lumberman, Edward Lammers, built his "Nonsuch" masterpiece (an architectual style named for Henry VIII's Nonsuch Palace in Surrey), the great green Victorian house at 1306 South Third, on Stillwater's South Hill. A three-story monument to a gilded age, it is carpenter's frenzy at its best, a flurry of superbly worked original detail proudly topped with improbable Viking ornaments.

William Sauntry, who had added iron ore speculation to his lumber interests, outdid Lammers by building a dazzling Moorish gymnasium behind his own mansion at 626 North Fourth on the opposing North Hill. Styled after the Spanish Alhambra, brightly painted and sumptuously appointed, its mirrored and columned ballroom was flanked by a reflective pool and a bowling alley. Sauntry also seems to have had the only tennis court in town.

Downtown, business blocks in brick and stone replaced earlier wooden frame structures and diversity was again the keynote. Wolf's Brewery, made of limestone dug in a Stillwater quarry, guarded the south end of town. A stranger might have taken it for a castle or fortress. Across the street, the three-story brick Grand Opera House went up where the Simonet Furniture Company now stands. Trimmed with Kasota stone, and definitely Queen Anne in spirit, a contemporary historian called it "the pride of the city and the finest opera house in the north-west." Kolliner's (men's and women's clothing) now occupies the ground floor of the Staples block, a stoic Romanesque structure much in keeping with the tastes of the man who built it.

Isaac Staples guided the town's fortunes for fifty years, making sure that Stillwater lived up to its potential. The mastermind of a lumbering empire, he owned huge tracts of prime pinelands to feed his sawmills. His large farms near Stillwater supplied his logging camps. He owned flour mills and retail stores. He was also president of the Lumberman's National Bank in Stillwater. While he prospered, so did Stillwater. When he died in his eighties in 1898, a boom era was ending.

Stillwater did herself up proud for this street fair in 1901. This photograph looks north on Main Street.

Few had seen the inevitable. The supply of choice timber and the demand for it were unlimited, most thought. In July, 1896, the *Mississippi Valley Lumberman* observed that "even today there is timber sufficient to keep the big saw mills at Stillwater and vicinity in operation for many years to come." But two years later that same paper conceded that the best days of lumbering on the St. Croix were over. It had taken the burly loggers little more than fifty years to strip Minnesota's centuries-old pine forests. Cut-over and burned-over wasteland scarred once timber-rich regions. By the turn of the century lumbermen were turning their sights to the Pacific Northwest. In 1914, with all the "old-timers" turned out for the occasion, the last log was officially floated through the St. Croix boom.

Stillwater was left choking on its own sawdust. By 1930, the town's population had dwindled by more than half. Nelle and Arthur Palmer had quit vaudeville to manage the new Lowell Inn, but they too were in trouble. Twin Citians, a lot of them unfamiliar with Stillwater, couldn't find the place.

Palmer came up with a novel solution. He painted the telephone poles blue and white along the county road from Minneapolis to Stillwater, then ordered newspaper advertising that told customers to follow the colorful guideposts to the inn. The telephone company took a dim view of the stunt, and Palmer ended up repainting its poles. But the Palmers, their flair for theatrics undaunted, became uncommonly successful innkeepers.

These record-breaking boards of select white pine, three feet wide and two-and-a-half inches thick, shown with employee Frank Stenlund, were cut in 1912 at David Tozer's sawmill in South Stillwater (which is now Bayport).

Nelle had been raised on the stage, playing cornet in her father's family band from the time she was five. Later, with a company in which Arthur played piano, she became the heroine of melodramas. When motion pictures became the rage, stage work was hard to come by, and the two decided they had learned enough about hotels through the years to run one.

The Palmers lived upstairs at the inn. It was the home Nelle had never had and she made it a showplace. Its antique furnishings were purchased reasonably during the Depression years. She insisted on English Spode and Wedgewood china for the George Washington dining room, and she picked up crystal goblets in different colors at estate sales. For birthdays and anniversaries, she and Arthur exchanged such things as silver candelabra and ornate serving pieces. Image was important to Nelle, her own as well as the inn's. She dressed flamboyantly in one-of-a-kind fashions, and played the role of Stillwater's grande dame to the hilt. Stillwater may have lost its lumbermen, but the Palmers and people like them who stayed kept the town alive and lively.

The Lowell Inn under construction on the site of the old Sawyer House, February 15, 1927.

Stillwater's Grand Opera House was the finest in the Northwest, built at a cost of $80,000 by four local businessmen, E. W. Durant, R. J. Wheeler, A. T. Jenks, and L. E. Torinus. Townspeople put on their fanciest dress and arrived in fashionable hacks and carriages for a gala opening performance, a Mason & Morgan production of "Uncle Tom's Cabin," on Saturday evening, May 14, 1881.

One hundred and one ornate gas fixtures lit its imposing auditorium, the walls were heavily frescoed, there was a large pipe organ on stage, and the drop curtain was painted with a scene from Louis XIV's garden at the Tuileries. More than twelve hundred people could be accomodated, half of these in the dress circle and the parquet. Lumberjacks and millworkers took up the "peanut gallery."

For twenty years, some of the top road troupes in the country played the Grand Opera House. John Philip Sousa brought his world-famous band to Stillwater. Prize fighters including John L. Sullivan appeared here. Between such engagements, home talent shows, political meetings, concerts, and lectures used the theatre.

Its builders had taken great pains to protect it against fire. Standing water pipes with attached hoses were installed in the wings and also in the galleries, and the entire house could be flooded in a few minutes time. Nevertheless, when a fire broke out in the theatre on the morning of December 5, 1902, it quickly burned to the ground. Volunteer fireman Frank Giossi said its entire front wall fell into Main Street in one piece. The Simonet Furniture Company's present store at 301 South Main is built atop its ashes.

Lumberman William Sauntry's private gymnasium included an opulent mirrored ballroom, a reflective pool, and a bowling alley.

The Lowell Park band poses in front of Joseph Wolf's brewery at the south end of Main Street for a summertime portrait in 1912. Joseph Wolf was born in Switzerland in 1832, and came to Stillwater with little else but "a brave heart and willing hands" in 1852. He married Mary Simonet five years later, and established the brewery in 1872.

Now the Stillwater Bakery, the building on the corner of Main and Chestnut was Byron Mosier's Cigar Store when this photograph was taken in 1915. Mosier had a side door in his place leading to the saloon next door that proved popular with businessmen who liked to imbibe discreetly during their noon lunch hours.

Mosier's Indian was one of the town's most popular citizens. Purchased in Chicago, he weighed 350 pounds, and except for his right arm and tomahawk, was carved from a single piece of pine. Men tipped their hats to him, townspeople posed beside him for their photographs, and at least one drunken lumberjack fled in terror after confronting him in the dark.

A Family Heirloom

Stillwater's a family town that has been passed down from generation to generation.

Eastons have been publishing the *Stillwater Gazette* since 1870. Theirs is the oldest family-owned daily-weekly newspaper in the state. Its founder, Augustus B. Easton came to Stillwater from Ohio in 1857 and worked first as a compositor for the *Stillwater Messenger,* which was then just a year old. Later in his career he edited a two-volume *History of the St. Croix Valley.* The *Gazette* moved to its present location at Second and Myrtle in 1904. The paper is currently run by Easton's great-great-grandson, John Easton.

Sebastian Simonet from Switzerland opened a cabinet-making shop in Stillwater in 1864. It was barely half a block from the present family-owned Simonet Furniture & Carpet Company. Sebastian also made caskets and that accounts for the Simonet Funeral Home, in business in Stillwater from the year of his arrival and owned and operated by his descendants.

Three generations of Mullers have made their living on the waterfront. George Muller was building steamboats in Stillwater in 1872. After the lumber industry died, Muller's sons made smaller boats—outboard rowboats, canoes, and racing boats. Now in the hands of his grandsons, Muller Boat Works, Inc. operates one of Stillwater's three marinas.

Uptown, where a thirsty populace once supported forty saloons, three generations of Meisters have been saloon keepers since 1898.

One family, now gone from Stillwater, became a legend. The Jeremys, father and son, were professional body-finders—fishers of corpses.

Sebastian Simonet in the doorway of his store with one of his ten children, Ludwig, about 1880.

The elder John Jeremy brought his wife and four children to Stillwater from St. Paul in the mid-1890s. His specialty was finding the bodies of drowning victims, and his success was uncanny. It was reported that he found up to three hundred bodies "from the Florida swamps to the lakes of Michigan and Illinois" with few failures.

He worked alone in his motorboat, sometimes staying on the water as long as twenty hours, and he allowed no onlookers. His fee was whatever he thought he could get—even going as high as $500. Once, when he was refused a $50 payment, he held the cadaver for ransom.

How he found the bodies was a matter of much local conjecture. "There ain't nothing wonderful about it," Fisherman John claimed. But townspeople thought differently. The guess was that he had trained muskrats in the mysterious gunnysack he always carried. Or perhaps a "body-compass" of his own devising. The newspapers insisted "there's some black art . . . somewhere. He's too good."

He came to a bizarre end. His wife left him, probably because he was a heavy drinker and a brawler. After that, he planned his own demise.

is was John Jeremy, Stillwater's professional
er of corpses.

On Saturday, July 20, 1918, he asked a Stillwater hardware merchant to draw up his will leaving everything including his gunnysack to his only son. He then boarded a streetcar for St. Paul where he had his shotgun repaired and bought buckshot shells. Returning to Stillwater, he purchased a white shirt from a local haberdasher. He wanted a good one, he said, because it would be his last. Next he paid a visit to the farm home of the girl who had lately been his housekeeper. About to be married, she had quit his employ and despite his entreaties, refused to return to him. When the girl's father ordered him off the property, Jeremy shot the farmer in cold blood, then made for a nearby wood where he took his own life with a blast to his head. The chief of police called the case one of unrequited love. The buckshot, he said, had been intended for the girl.

Jeremy's son, also named John, took up where his father had left off. More talkative than his father, he maintained he had no secrets. "I am a fisherman just as my father was," he told a reporter in 1921. "I find the bodies of drowned people, as my father did also." This younger Jeremy brought up nearly five hundred bodies. It was nothing but "honest, horny-handed work," he said.

A neighbor divulged the contents of the soggy gunnysack. "There weren't no trained muskrats or anything like that," he confided. "It was a bunch of lead pipes with three-pronged hooks at the end. When he attached 'em to a line he covered every inch of the ground that way. His secret was patience."

arl Meister's "German Band" posed for John unk on Main Street on July 1, 1936. Runk entified the musicians from left to right as ene Hansen, Laurence Scramstad, Adolph ary, Earl Palmer, Carl Meister, William rueger, Sherman Wick, and George Palmer.

There were numerous hotels and boarding houses in Stillwater in sawmill days when hundreds of single working men needed to be housed and fed. The Keystone House on the south side of West Myrtle at Fourth, pictured here about 1880, catered to a "better class of boarders," young bachelor business and professional men.

John Runk took this photo of George H. Atwood in the taxidermy workshop of his museum about 1910. The museum was housed in the private gymnasium at the lumberman's home at 320 West Pine. Built in the 1890s, the gymnasium was one of the finest of its kind in the country, and included "every mechanical device known to athletics," a bowling alley, and a fully-equipped observatory.

Atwood was one of Stillwater's most successful lumbermen. He was a partner with Frederick Weyerhaeuser and William Sauntry in the Atwood Lumber Company at Willow River, Minnesota. He also eventually ended up with both the original Hersey and Staples, and the Schulenberg and Boeckeler sawmills. It was Atwood's idea to bring timber into Stillwater by rail. In 1894, his "A" mill (the former Hersey, Staples property) was the first in the St. Croix Valley to receive logs—five million feet that year—by this means of transportation.

The Town's on the Rebound

Stillwater is currently one of the fastest growing communities in the state. Its population now exceeds thirteen thousand, an increase of four thousand persons during the last decade. Its economy is thriving.

Two reasons are apparent. Improved highway access to the Twin Cities has made it a commuters' haven. Stillwater's appeal, though, has been in her well-timed return to the past. For what it's worth, the turnabout in Stillwater's fortunes occurred precisely when the city stopped tearing down its old buildings and started sandblasting and revamping what it had. Renewed pride in the city's history has played a key role in its rejuvenation.

Preservation has become a popular platform. One public action group saved Stillwater's county courthouse, the first in the state, to convert it into a center for the arts. Another group is surveying the city's historic buildings to ensure their survival. Private investors are gambling heavily on the renewal.

Jerry Perkl was one of the first to see the commercial potential in Stillwater's vintage structures. He bought the 1880s Stillwater Motors building, originally a rooming house, and began transforming it into his Grand Garage and Gallery on Main Street in 1970. Gutting its interior, he built in a collection of specialty shops using carefully selected architectural treasures.

The Garage became a Stillwater landmark thanks to Perkl, but it is no longer his. He lost it when his White Bear Dodge dealership went bankrupt and the Chrysler Credit Corporation foreclosed on the Stillwater property. An investment group, Darius & Associates, purchased the Grand Garage in 1980 and is completing its rehabilitation.

The Adolphus C. Hospes house at 303 North Fourth Street, currently owned by booksellers James and Kristen Cummings. Hospes was a prosperous merchant, born in Missouri in 1841. He moved to Stillwater with his family as a youth when his father came here to supervise the building of the Schulenberg and Boeckeler mill in 1854. Hospes served several years as secretary of the St. Croix Boom Company, and was married to Isaac Staples's daughter, Aurora. The house reportedly harbors the ghost of Staples.

One man was killed and several others injured when scaffolding inside Stillwater's courthouse collapsed during its construction in 1868. According to historian James Taylor Dunn, bricklayer Henry Ghostley died immediately after being "catapulted some fifty feet over the wall, turning two somersaults in mid-air and landing squarely on his head."

Stillwater's historic Washington County Courthouse is the oldest in Minnesota. It was designed by Augustus F. Knight, St. Paul's first resident architect, who also designed General William Le Duc's house in Hastings. Replete with period cupola, its stately Italianate facade mirrors the confident era that produced it.

More recent suitors have fared better.

Bob Sabes from Minneapolis (owner of the Rainbow Cafe at Lake and Hennepin) speculated on a derelict railroad building and came up with his winning Freight House restaurant and Water Street Saloon. In 1981, he added Croix Country for country music lovers in the same building. Before Sabes started his renovation, there had been talk of tearing the building down and diverting traffic off Main Street and through the railroad property to the interstate bridge. It has since been placed on the National Historic Register.

Cy and Mary Ann Turnbladh operate Tamarack House Galleries, one of the Midwest's largest and best-known art galleries, in a former NSP office building on Main Street.

Across the street, local architect Mike McGuire fashioned his Brick Alley complex, two buildings separated by an alley but connected by a "bridge," from an outmoded NSP coal degasification plant. McGuire is also responsible for the Second Street Store. A young bridegroom built this brick house in 1846, but his wife took one look at the size of it and refused to move in. McGuire's use of the structure appears to be more appropriate.

Eleven years ago, when they came here from Vermont, Norm and Jean Davis bought the "great green" Lammers house. (To their surprise, it *was* the "rare architectural masterpiece" the newspaper ad had promised!) They're the ones who dreamed up a second life for the old post office across from Lowell Inn at Second and Myrtle. Built in 1905, this Beaux Arts beauty is making the most of its reincarnation as the Old Post Office Shops.

Brine's Old Fashioned Meats, run by the Brine family on Main Street, has been in business in Stillwater since 1958, but the three-story building it occupies was owned and operated as a grocery and general store in the 1860s by Isaac Staples in partnership with lumberman Louis Torinus.

At the north end of town, Monty Brine, with his wife, Terri, and Bruce and Diane Rollie have converted what remains of Isaac Staples's long-abandoned sawmill into Staples Mill Antiques, with space for more than thirty dealers who specialize in everything from Victorian furniture to maritime antiques.

This is O. A. Anderson's Lunch Room on East Chestnut Street in Stillwater in 1912. Pictured left to right are Albert (Shorty) Leonard, John Dolan, Arthur Olson, and Dick Dolan.

Stillwater was born a hustler. There's never been any doubt about that. But everybody knows time ran out for her just past the turn of the century. Everybody except Stillwater. Up to her old tricks, plying her old-fashioned wiles, this lumbermen's mistress is cashing in on her gaudy past.

Her history is suddenly her most valuable asset, her extravagant period architecture her trump card. After decades as a wallflower, she's being courted by present-day entrepreneurs who are reveling in her refurbishing. King Pine once paid her way. Now the tourists do.

The town's in the midst of a new boom that has everything to do with nostalgia. A riverfront queen back in favor, her waters are crowded with pleasure craft, and her downtown streets a bustling collage of well-peopled shops and eateries. Lumberjack Days in mid-summer relive her golden years in rollicking pageantry. Gussied up in new-bought fancy-dress finery, Stillwater's a Victorian charmer out to make the most of a second go-around.

This book ends with an enormous, if belated, thank you to John Runk who cared enough to make it possible. Few cities have had such colorful yesterdays as Stillwater. Fewer still can boast a hometown photographer who so faithfully preserved them.

Victorian at heart, Runk preserved this carefully-arranged view of one of his studios, complete with weasel skins on the lace curtains.

Notes

James Taylor Dunn's book, *The St. Croix*, first published in 1965, is the best (and only comprehensive) popular history of the St. Croix Valley. I recommend it highly. Basic histories of the area include *Fifty Years in the Northwest* by lumberman William H. C. Folsom, 1888, *History of Washington County and the St. Croix Valley* edited by George E. Warner and Charles M. Foote, 1881, and *History of the St. Croix Valley* edited by Augustus B. Easton, 1909.

In addition to these, the sources I used included Agnes Larson's *History of the White Pine Industry in Minnesota*, 1949, *Timber and Men* by Ralph Hidy, Frank Ernest Hill, and Allan Nevins, 1963, *A Raft Pilot's Log* by Walter Blair, 1930, *Looking Backward* by E. L. Roney, 1970, and *Washington: A History of the Minnesota County*, published by the Washington County Historical Society in 1977. Area newspapers, of course, were extremely helpful, and numerous Stillwater residents provided information concerning their families and themselves for this book.

Acknowledgements

The idea for this book was conceived while I was writing an article about Stillwater which appeared in *Twin Cities* magazine (April, 1981). John Hodowanic, the magazine's editor, also edited this book. I deeply appreciate your help, John.

I would also like to thank several other people who contributed significantly to the success of this project.

Dale Johnston designed the book. He was my husband's classmate at the Minneapolis College of Art and Design, and is a partner with us in Johnston Publishing, Inc. He also guided the book through production. Because of him, I am immensely proud of it.

Sue Collins at the Stillwater Public Library answered countless research questions for me. She also read the final manuscript and her corrections have saved me much embarrassment. I'm grateful, too, to Diane Thompson of Stillwater who shared her voluminous research material concerning Isaac Staples with me, to Polly Webster, president of Stillwater's library board, and to Louise Johnson, curator of the Washington County Historical Museum. Bonnie Wilson at the Minnesota Historical Society was also especially helpful.

My husband, Charlie, photographed John Runk's photographs for this book at the Stillwater Public Library and the Minnesota Historical Society. More than that, his enthusiastic support of this venture has made the work a delight. He has provided me with a comfortable library of my own in which to work, and has cheerfully read and reread manuscript, making many valuable suggestions. For these and more personal reasons, this book is dedicated to him.

The passenger boat Verne Swain *was built in Stillwater by the Swain boatworks which built and operated many of the steamers on the St. Croix and Mississippi rivers.*

Index

100 ✻

Frank McGray, shown on the right, hitches the last log to go through the St. Croix boom, on June 12, 1914. McGray is also said to have sent the first log through the new boom in 1856, and for many years was superintendent at the boom. His field office was a rowboat, equipped with an oarsman, from which he kept close watch on booming operations.

The Boom Site, two miles above Stillwater on Highway 95, is now on the National Register of Historic Places and serves as a roadside park. The boom company's "settlement" here once numbered some twenty buildings, including two frame dormitories. Except for McGray's house across the highway, now a private home, all of these are gone.

This book was designed by Dale K. Johnston. The production consultant was Rohland W. Wiltfang. The type style used throughout the book is Palatino. Paper for the text is Warrenflo Gloss. The book was printed by Kolorpress, Inc.